Thank you for purchasing this by RAKA Custom. Japan is a fascinating country, steeped in culture and traditions, thousands of years old. Many of which are still practised to this day. It is a country rich in culture, a place where you are never too far from the wonders it holds. This book explores and reveals many of the wonders, the rich and diverse culture, the incredible natural beauty and the infamous architecture. I very much hope you enjoy these exceptional images as much as I do. Enjoy and Arigatōgozaimashita

Kanji (漢字)

Kanji is one if several scripts used in traditional Japanese writing styles. "Kanji" literally means "Han characters" or "Chinese characters" and it is identical to the characters in China to describe their writing. Kanji are mainly used to describe names and nouns.

Some other Script style include:

Hiragana (平仮名) and Katakana (片仮名). The Japanese also use Hentaigana (変体仮名) a set of archaic and almost obsolete Kana.

Temples (寺, tera)

Temples (寺, tera) Are the places of worship in Japanese Buddhism. Virtually every Japanese municipality has at least one temple, while large cultural centers like Kyoto have several hundred.
The oldest of the Japanese temples is Hōryū-ji, (法隆寺, Temple of the Flourishing Dharma). The temple was founded by Prince Shōtoku in 607 and is widely recognised as the oldest wooden building in the world.
One of Japans most famous temples is Kinkaku-ji, (金閣寺, literally "Temple of the Golden Pavilion"), Nobody is allowed inside and the top two floors are covered in gold leaf. (See overleaf)

Daruma Dolls 達磨

Daruma dolls are modelled after Bodhidharma, the founder of Zen Buddhism. Daruma dolls originated in the city of Takasaki, around the mid 1760s. They are a hollow Papiermâché doll and often have a wooden mold to create their shape.

Architecture

(日本建築, Nihon kenchiku)
Japan is home to some of the
worlds most intricate and
fascinating architecture From
Temples to buildings, shrines to
statues. You are never far away
from something that will catch
your eye. Traditional Japanese
architecture incorporates wood,
screen and sliding doors, tatami (
畳), verandas, Genkan (玄関)
and it incorporates with
surrounding nature. This can be
seen by the way natural light is
used in older buildings as well as
the use of wood, in its raw form.

Cheery Blossoms Sakura (桜)

The Sakura or Cherry Blossoms of Japan are famous worldwide. Your best chance of seeing them full bloom is in late March to early April. Not just a beautiful flower, they are tied into the very fabric of Japanese history. Originally used to divine the years coming harvest, they also embody Wabi-sabi philosophy and shinto ideals of impermanence, hope and renewal.

Natural Beauty

Japan is a treasure trove of things to see and do. At the very top of that list are natural beauty spots and parks. one of the most prominent being the Shinjuku Gyoen National Garden. A place that has offered a green refuge since the Edo period.

Culture

Japan is a country rich in culture From the Geisha (芸者) to Origami (折り紙,), to Shinto priests(神主), Ikebana (生け花, 活け花) and the Samurai (侍). Arts and religions practised for thousands of years that still live on today.

Restaurant & Nightlife

There are literally thousands of restaurants in all major Japanese cities. You will not struggle to find a place to eat. That said if you really want to experience Japanese culture, take yourself off the Main streets and look for little doors that lead to restaurants. You can get a bento box type meal in a side street in for less than £10.

Aside from working hard, being honourable and very polite. The Japanese are also known to let their hair down regularly. Most major cities are filled with bustling nightspots to get a drink or some food. You can even find English and Irish themed pubs. Lets not forget the incredible robot show in Tokyo.

Breath-taking views

Most countries are know for a famous landmark or two, but Japan is a country with an abundance of exceptional buildings, beauty spots and scenic views, that in an instant can take your breath away.
From the temples and shrines to the statues and gardens.
Japan is a country second to none for eye catching scenery.

Thank you for joining me on this journey through these beautiful Images of Japan. Japan is one of the most incredible countries on earth. It is a country that once you have visited, you will leave a piece of your heart with it. If you haven't already booked your flight, then Hayaku (早く). Arigatōgozaimashita and Ki hajimekai (期一会).

Printed in Great Britain
by Amazon

35868650R00053